CLASSIC ROCK BANDS

THE WHO

by Sue Bradford Edwards

CONTENT CONSULTANT

Jack Hamilton
Assistant Professor
Media Studies and
American Studies
University of Virginia

An Imprint of Abdo Publishing | abdobooks.com

abdobooks.com

Published by Abdo Publishing, a division of ABDO, PO Box 398166, Minneapolis, Minnesota 55439. Copyright © 2022 by Abdo Consulting Group, Inc. International copyrights reserved in all countries. No part of this book may be reproduced in any form without written permission from the publisher. Essential Library™ is a trademark and logo of Abdo Publishing.

Printed in the United States of America, North Mankato, Minnesota.
052021
092021

Cover Photo: AP Images
Interior Photos: Pictorial Press Ltd/Alamy, 4–5, 10–11, 38–39, 88–89; Jack Fordyce/Shutterstock Images, 12; Everett Historical/Shutterstock Images, 14–15; Shutterstock Images, 18; GAB Archive/Redferns/Getty Images, 21; Cyrus Andrews/Michael Ochs Archives/Getty Images, 24–25; Mario De Biasi/ Mondadori Portfolio/Getty Images, 26–27; AP Images, 30, 74–75, 79, 91; Monitor Picture Library/Photoshot/Hulton Archive/Getty Images, 34; André Crudo/Photo 12/Alamy, 37; Chris Morphet/Redferns/Getty Images, 42, 52–53; Bruce Fleming/AP Images, 46; Steve Wood/Express/Hulton Archive/Getty Images, 48–49; Steve Starr/AP Images, 56–57; Gijsbert Hanekroot/Alamy, 58–59; David Hickes/Alamy, 62; David Redfern/Redferns/Getty Images, 67; PictureLux/The Hollywood Archive/Alamy, 68–69; Barrett/Mirrorpix/Newscom, 77; Mirrorpix/Newscom, 80–81; Brian Horton/AP Images, 86; Anthony Mooney/ Shutterstock Images, 95

Editor: Melissa York
Series Designer: Colleen McLaren

Library of Congress Control Number: 2019954360

Publisher's Cataloging-in-Publication Data

Names: Edwards, Sue Bradford, author.
Title: The Who / by Sue Bradford Edwards
Description: Minneapolis, Minnesota : Abdo Publishing, 2022 | Series: Classic rock bands | Includes online resources and index.
Identifiers: ISBN 9781532192043 (lib. bdg.) | ISBN 9781532179945 (ebook)
Subjects: LCSH: The Who (Musical group)--Juvenile literature. | Rock and roll bands--Biography--Juvenile literature. | Rock musicians--Great Britain--Biography--Juvenile literature. | Psychedelic rock music--Juvenile literature.
Classification: DDC 782.42166--dc23

CONTENTS

CHAPTER ONE

Destruction

Inside the dimly lit Railway Hotel and Club in Harrow, England, the mod crowd danced shoulder to shoulder. Mod was a British teen subculture. Boys wore narrow trousers and tight long-sleeved soccer shirts. A few sported dark suit jackets and narrow ties. Girls wore tailored, knee-length dresses, their straight hair swinging in time to the music. Occasionally a cigarette flared in the dark.

Like other bands playing clubs in September 1964, the Who performed R&B songs made popular by other groups. Many bands, including the Who, have started their careers by playing covers of other people's music and gaining fans before working on

When the Who was playing in English clubs in 1964, they wore clothes in the mod style.

Premier
THE

their own songs. On this night, the Who played R&B classics including "Smokestack Lightning" by Howlin' Wolf and "I'm a Man" and "Road Runner," both by Bo Diddley. The band's members looked like the club's patrons, and they put on a great show.

Lead singer Roger Daltrey sometimes played the harmonica or kept rhythm with maracas. The Rock & Roll Hall of Fame later called Daltrey a natural front man. From actively swinging the mike to energetically moving around the stage, Daltrey put on a good show for audiences while passionately singing in a style the Hall of Fame would one day say "embodied the muscular power of the band's music."[1]

John Entwistle kept time on his bass, a mellow counterpoint to Daltrey's energy. Keith Moon moved constantly behind his drum kit,

The High Numbers

When the band played the Railway Hotel, it was called the High Numbers, a name recommended by manager Pete Meaden. Meaden believed the name the Who was "too ethereal, too abstract, too airy-fairy to connect."[2] Would-be fans needed a name that told them something about the band, and High Numbers was a nod to amphetamines, one of the most popular street drugs at that time. The members of the band didn't like the new name, but Meaden assured them that a better name was part of reaching the top of the charts when they recorded their own music.

flailing his arms, tossing and catching his sticks, and standing up to play. Guitarist Pete Townshend sometimes strummed the guitar by windmilling his arm in huge circles. Other times he would bang the instrument into the speaker stack or hold it high overhead.

Rather than letting the guitar hinder his movement, Townshend used it to enlarge his stage presence. The long-necked instrument extended his reach as he thrust it out and up. When he did this in front of an amplifier, also known as an amp, feedback squealed from the speakers. Townshend employed the howling wails of feedback in the Who's music, raising the sound levels until the band could shake the walls of smaller venues like the Railway Hotel. Townshend also developed a guitar style that emphasized the rhythm of the song by striking chords in time to the beat.

Windmill Whammy

Townshend's windmill technique isn't without risk. He admits that he often tears off fingernails, but it can be much worse. On August 16, 1989, at a performance in Tacoma, Washington, the guitarist windmilled while playing "Won't Get Fooled Again" and felt a stabbing pain. He had impaled his hand on the guitar's tremolo bar, also called the whammy bar. This slim metal piece protrudes from the front of the guitar and pierced his hand between two bones. The injury sent him to the hospital, but there was no permanent damage and he played the next performance.

With Townshend sometimes picking up the rhythm in his guitar lines, Entwistle experimented with his bass guitar. Instead of playing quietly in the background, as do many bass players, he played louder and used wire-wrapped strings that vibrated in a way that resulted in a more complex sound. Entwistle created a more pronounced sound that resembled a second lead guitar. Before the Who, the drummer also played a background role, but Moon wasn't willing to take a back seat. He did more than mark the beat of the song, laying in additional percussion that often gave the effect of two drum sets being played simultaneously.

"It's really still funny to this day when we do a song with John doing a blinding bass run . . . and I'm just standing there plucking away and they wonder how I do it."[3]

– Pete Townshend, on people believing he played Entwistle's solos

ICONIC ACCIDENT

In preparation for the performance at the Railway Hotel, the band built its own extensions over the original stage. This raised the four musicians higher above the crowd for easy visibility, but it also brought them closer to the ceiling. Holding the guitar overhead in front of the speaker stack produced feedback, part of the band's signature stage routine.

When Townshend thrust his guitar upward, the instrument thumped into the ceiling. This hadn't been intentional, but after it happened once, Townshend repeated the movement, striking the ceiling several times.

Eventually, the guitar's long neck snapped. "There were a few laughs. . . . Everyone was waiting for me to kind of sob over my guitar. . . . That'll teach you to be flash. . . . I had no recourse but to completely look as though I meant to do it, so I smashed the guitar and jumped all over the bits," Townshend later said.[4]

Feedback

When an electric guitar is held in front of an amp, the sound from the amp vibrates the guitar strings. The amp translates those vibrations into amplified sound. That sound then vibrates the guitar's strings, the vibrations are picked up, and they become more amplified sound. The process repeats, creating a screeching sound known as feedback. Feedback has become part of modern rock.

The next time the band played the Railway Hotel, the crowd wanted to see Townshend smash another guitar. When he didn't, some people left. Moon got mad and knocked over his drums. Word of Moon's stunt spread, and at the band's next Railway Hotel performance, a larger crowd showed up. This time both Townshend and Moon broke their instruments. Drumheads are cheaper to replace than full guitars.

Smashing guitars became an iconic aspect of the Who's performances.

Kit Lambert, the band's British record producer, was initially horrified when Townshend and then Moon destroyed instruments and equipment. Lambert worried that the violence would alienate fans who had never seen anything like this. Lambert

wasn't alone in his negative response. When Townshend first smashed a guitar, Daltrey argued the broken instrument could have been repaired when it only had a snapped neck. Entwistle couldn't believe a musician would treat his instrument like

The Who were still putting on energetic performances for fans more than 50 years after the band's debut.

that, but Lambert and the group eventually realized that they could sell the band's energy, anger, and destruction. Although destruction became one of the band's trademarks, that part of the Who's identity alone wouldn't have taken them from Britain to the United States and around the world. Many bands, including those that inspired the Who, have faded from memory, but the Who are still performing and thrilling audiences.

Destruction

When asked about smashing his guitar, Townshend said, "I justified it in terms of being noticed."[5] Moon saw things differently and said they were angry because they had exhausted themselves to get the song perfect but got no response from the crowd. "That's when the f****** instruments go," Moon said.[6] Biographer Dave Marsh noted that whichever perspective is correct, the drive to make this destruction part of the act came from the fans who demanded to see it happen again.

"We were probably the most aggressive group that's ever happened in England."[7]

– Roger Daltrey

CHAPTER TWO

The Beginning

The members of the Who grew up in Britain during a frugal time when the country was struggling to rebuild. During World War II (1939–1945), the Germans bombed London and other British cities. Incendiary bombs set fires, and rockets brought down buildings while people hid in shelters, never knowing what they would find when the bombing stopped.

Daltrey was born on March 1, 1944, in West London during a bombing raid. When his father was drafted, Daltrey and his mother, like many Londoners, were evacuated and sent to live in the countryside. The two spent the rest of the war on a

A relentless German bombing campaign left British cities in ruins during World War II. The members of the Who grew up in the aftermath of this destruction.

Scottish farm, sharing a four-room farmhouse with the owner, another farm family, and some relatives.

By the end of the war, Britain had been devastated. More than 60,000 civilians had been killed, approximately 85,000 more were injured, and more than one million homes were destroyed.[1] World War II cost Britain an enormous amount of money, and the British felt the impact of this debt and destruction for years. Townshend and his friends played in bomb sites and found human bones. Many children who had been evacuated were bullied, and some had been abused. When children tried to discuss the things that had happened to them, they were often told to be grateful they had survived. This silence, says biographer Ben Marshall, was something the members of the Who refused to accept. Eventually, they found their voices through music.

Beyond the Stiff Upper Lip

The British attitude in the mid-1900s was sometimes called "keeping a stiff upper lip." It meant that no one, not even children, could complain about things that happened during and after World War II. Townshend wrote about this in "1921," one of the songs in the rock opera *Tommy*. When young Tommy sees a murder committed, his parents tell him again and again that he saw nothing and heard nothing. "You won't say nothing to no one."[2] The toddler not only keeps silent about the murder but literally sees, hears, and says nothing for years.

THE DETOURS

Daltrey, Townshend, and Entwistle attended West London's Acton County Grammar School together. Townshend and Entwistle had a similar sense of humor and loved New Orleans–style jazz, so they went to shows whenever they could. Daltrey arrived at Acton because of his good test scores. The school, though still working class, seemed too posh to Daltrey, who was accustomed to a rougher area. Townshend and Entwistle would see Daltrey and vice versa, but they didn't really know each other while at Acton. Unlike the other students, Daltrey's main interest was rock music. Instead of studying, he got into fights, caused trouble in class, and skipped school, which got him expelled in 1959 on his fifteenth birthday. Next, Daltrey worked a series of

Growing Up with Music

John Entwistle was born on October 9, 1944, in West London. His parents divorced shortly thereafter, and he grew up in his grandmother's home. When he was seven, his father taught him to play trumpet and piano. Entwistle disliked piano, but in playing it he learned to read and write music. Pete Townshend was born May 19, 1945, in West London. His father was a saxophone player in the Royal Air Force Dance Band and his mother sang with two orchestras. They were heavy drinkers and fought often. Townshend was bullied at school for his large nose, and home brought no relief, as his mother also mocked him. Still, like Entwistle, he followed his family into music.

Daltrey wrote about his early life in his 2018 memoir, *Thanks a Lot Mr Kibblewhite.*

menial jobs, including at a sheet-metal shop where he brought the other workers tea and sandwiches and sanded the welds that joined pieces of metal to make computer cases. It was just a job—a way to earn the money he needed to build a guitar.

When he was 12, Daltrey had built a flimsy plywood guitar that fell apart in only six weeks. Later his uncle, a carpenter, helped him build his second guitar, creating a strong connection between the neck and the body and applying polish. The sound wasn't perfect, but it looked good and held together.

In 1961, Daltrey formed a skiffle band called the Detours. Skiffle took musical inspiration from New Orleans blues and jazz. Daltrey's band included Harry Wilson on drums, Reggie Chaplin on bass, Colin Dawson on vocals, and Ian Moody. Moody was the face, a good-looking, well-dressed leader who made the band appear cool. Not surprisingly, Daltrey played the guitar.

At this time, Entwistle was a member of the Scorpions with Townshend, who played guitar. Entwistle played the trumpet at first but switched to bass, playing an instrument he made himself. He was carrying this bass home from practice when he ran into Daltrey. Daltrey invited him to a rehearsal, and Entwistle eventually joined the Detours. When the Detours' then guitar player, Roy Ellis, drowned in 1962, Townshend, who was by then a student at Ealing Art College, replaced him.

Entwistle and Townshend were intimidated by Daltrey because the young sheet-metal worker was one of the toughest teddy boys in West London. Teddy boys, or teds, were working-class teens who adopted the fashionable clothing of the upper class of the early 1900s. But teddy boys weren't all about clothes. They also liked to fight. He wasn't the best musician in the group, but Daltrey's word was law, and he backed it up with his fists when necessary.

The Teddy Boys

Easily recognized by their narrow-legged trousers and loosely draped coats, the working-class teddy boys took these upper-class styles and made them their own, abandoning white shirts and gray or black jackets for bright blues and pinks. They also added American string ties. Girls wore tailored jackets over slim trousers, pencil skirts, or widely flared poodle skirts with flat shoes. The group latched onto American rock and roll. Many teds just wanted to look good, but others loved to fight, forming gangs and rioting. The teds were the original British teen subculture, leading the way for rockers, mods, and more.

THE ROLLING STONES

In December 1963, the Detours played at Saint Mary's Hall with the Rolling Stones, a soon-to-be-famous rock band that was just getting more popular. The bands played similar cover songs, a variety

The band that eventually became the Who began as the Detours in 1961.

of R&B songs by artists including Muddy Waters, Jimmy Reed, and Howlin' Wolf, but the two bands had very different looks. The Detours wore their hair neatly trimmed with white shirts, dark trousers, and ties, while the Rolling Stones sported long hair and disheveled clothing. They were, according to Townshend, a stylish mess. He said, "I learned more rock 'n' roll theater that night than any other."[3]

This was when Townshend first saw a guitarist windmill his arm. The Rolling Stones' Keith Richards did it before the show to warm up. Townshend liked the look of the move but didn't want to copy

> "We were scheduled to support the Rolling Stones in Putney at the end of December 1963 and I was prepared to be cynical; without hearing them play, I'd decided their reputation must be based on their hairstyles. Instead I was blown away."[4]
>
> *– Townshend on meeting the Rolling Stones, 2012*

something so unique. Several weeks later, they again played with the Rolling Stones. When Richards didn't windmill in warm-up, Townshend realized it wasn't something the other guitarist did regularly and decided to make the move his own. Townshend soon had the opportunity to show this move off as lead guitarist. Daltrey's filing job, for which he used a metal file to smooth rough edges on recently welded sheet metal, meant he always had cut fingers. It made guitar work painful, so he turned the role over to Townshend.

JOHNNY DEVLIN AND THE DETOURS

Early in 1964, the band Johnny Devlin and the Detours appeared on the television show *Thank Your Lucky Stars*. There could be only one band called the Detours, so Daltrey, Entwistle, and Townshend needed to find a new name. They gathered at Townshend's flat with his roommate, Richard Barnes. Because newspapers constantly talked about the length of teens' hair, Townshend suggested the Hair, but none of the Detours had long hair. Barnes proposed the Who, which had a quick, punchy sound. Townshend then suggested the Hair and the Who, but everyone went home without reaching a decision.

As often happened with the band at this time, Daltrey settled the matter. When he arrived to pick Townshend up the next morning, he greeted Barnes. "It's the Who, innit?"[5]

The Who's lineup was not yet in its final form. They were still missing Keith Moon. The Detours' drummer was Doug Sandom, who was 15 years older than the other members of the band. He was a solid drummer, but his age was keeping them from getting a record deal—executives said he was too old. So, even though everyone liked Sandom, he played with the band for the last time on April 13, 1964.

Making Moon

Keith Moon was born at Central Middlesex Hospital in northwestern London on August 23, 1946. His father was a mechanic, and his mother worked part time as a cleaner. Both were quiet people. Unlike the other members of the band, Moon flunked his Eleven-plus exams, which meant he could not continue on the same academic route as those who passed the test. Starting at 15 years old, Moon worked menial jobs, including one at a printshop. At 16, his father bought him a drum set, and Moon learned quickly, taking lessons and also playing along to records.

By the mid-1960s, the name and lineup of the Who had solidified.

The group used a temporary drummer while they searched for a replacement.

They found their permanent replacement drummer about the same time they had to rename the band. The Who was on break while

playing a show when someone introduced them to Moon. They agreed to let him play two songs with them and realized the energetic drummer's unconventional style was just what they needed.

CHAPTER THREE

The Mods

Like teddy boys, British mods belonged to a teen subculture. They grew up after World War II and saw their parents save, make do without much money, and work long hours. They wanted to live differently than their parents and started by spending the money they earned on clothes and scooters. They chose tailored Italian garments, including fitted dresses and jackets worn with light-colored trousers and American military parkas. They motored on Italian scooters produced by Vespa or Lambretta. They gravitated to modern music, beginning with jazz and later adding groups, like the Who, that developed from jazz

The mod subculture featured a distinctive sense of fashion.

and R&B. These working-class teens were tired of being told how they should act.

Pete Meaden, one of the most influential mods, was a face that others looked to for his opinions on music and style. He had worked as a publicist with American musician Chuck Berry in addition to the Rolling Stones. Although Daltrey was a ted, Meaden decided to shape the Who into the perfect mods. Onstage, the band reflected the audience's anger at society.

Mod Style

Although Meaden chose the Who for his mod makeover, they did not initially look the part. A mod had to have mod clothes, mod hair, and a mod scooter. Meaden took the Who to the barber. Daltrey already had a mod haircut, but the others were given French crew cuts, short on the sides, long and combed back on top. Entwistle didn't argue, but as soon as they left the barber, he combed his hair forward. The Who were never entirely mod in part because they were slightly older than their mod audience, but also because they had bigger goals than just appealing to one youth subculture. They wanted to make it big.

MOD ENERGY AND DRIVE

On Easter weekend, March 28 and 29, 1964, up to 1,000 young people from London arrived in the British seaside town of Clacton.[1] So early in the spring season, little was open in this tourist destination, and the weather was bad. Because the young people had nothing to do, fights between mods and another subculture, rockers, erupted around town. Although both groups wanted to break away from the dominant culture, they were so intolerant of people who were different from themselves that they came into conflict with each other.

Afterward, newspapers carried headlines like "Day of Terror by Scooter Groups" in the *Daily Telegraph* and "Wild Ones Invade Seaside—97 Arrests" in the *Daily Mirror*.[2] Even though the papers exaggerated events, soon more rockers and mods wanted in on the action and excitement. Between May 16 and 18, 1964, approximately 1,000 young people from London arrived in the seaside town of Brighton. Again, they fought, and 76 people were arrested in what newspapers dubbed "The Battle of Brighton."[3]

Rockers

The rockers were another British subculture. Whereas mods were neatly tailored, rockers wore jeans, white T-shirts, leather boots, and leather jackets. They rode motorcycles instead of scooters, and their music of choice was American rock and roll. Like mods, they wanted to be unique and different from the dominant culture.

Journalists Charles Hamblett and Jane Deverson wrote *Generation X*, a book on youth culture. They interviewed participants, including John Braden, an

Clashes involving mods and other youth subcultures would be referenced in later music by the Who.

18-year-old London mechanic. "It was like we were taking over the country. You want to hit back at all the old geezers who try to tell us what to do. We just want to show them we're not going to take it," Braden said.[4]

Meaden believed the Who could take advantage of this mod desire to stand apart from society. The first step was selecting a mod name. Meaden claimed the name the Who wouldn't last more than a year and renamed the band the High Numbers. Next, Meaden wrote two mod songs for them to record. "I'm the Face" and "Zoot Suit," named for a suit style worn by male mods, were full of mod slang. Although Meaden bought 50 copies and even Entwistle's grandmother purchased one, the record sold only 500 copies, in part because the songs were unoriginal. "I'm the Face" imitated Slim Harpo's "I Got Love If You Want It," while "Zoot Suit" mirrored the Dynamics' "Misery." Mods wanted more than a mod veneer.

> "I had this dream of getting a group together that would be the focus, the entertainers for the mods, a group that would actually be the same people on stage as the guys in the audience."[5]
>
> *– Pete Meaden about his work with the Who, 1975*

MAKING MUSIC

By November 1964, the embarrassed band had replaced Meaden as manager with Kit Lambert and Chris Stamp. Townshend was again composing their music, and they again called themselves the Who. To bring fans to the band's shows, Lambert and Stamp gave out fliers at pubs and clubs. They also recruited a group of mods to come to the shows. Influential mods, the faces others would follow to a new club or to a new band, got in for

Mod Lingo

As with every subculture, mods spoke their own language, and it went far beyond whether someone was a *face* or a *ticket*—a mod who's trying too hard or one who's just a bit behind fashion. A *seven and six* was someone who wore cheap off-the-rack clothes that looked like mod fashions. *Deck* meant to mock someone, perhaps a seven and six. *Jumping through* someone meant fighting them, as in jumping through a ticket who decked you. And if you decked someone really well? It was the biggest thrill, or *flashkick*.

free, and other recruits got in at half price. Within three weeks, the Who's Tuesday night gigs at the Marquee Club were breaking attendance records.

Lambert and Stamp also got the Who a recording contract with producer Shel Talmy. When the band arrived at the studio to record the single "I Can't Explain," it found Talmy's musicians ready to play. One of them was Jimmy Page, later of Led Zeppelin, who replaced Townshend on lead guitar for part of the song. Using session musicians is common, but it is hard for a musician like Townshend to be replaced in performing his own music. Talmy told Daltrey to sing light and easy.

Talmy's methods produced success. The opening riff of "I Can't Explain" is raw and powerful, leading it to become a regular show starter for the band. This song became the first of several pop hits for the Who.

Lambert and Stamp had an additional goal: to get the band on the pop show *Ready Steady Go!* Fortunately, Lambert knew the show's producer. The Who joined *Ready Steady Go!* host Cathy McGowan on January 29, 1965. Lambert flooded the studio audience with Who fans, and to viewers it appeared that the band was at the head of its own mod mob.

For more publicity, Lambert got Townshend interviews in newspapers, magazines, and radio, and the guitarist discussed his desire to tear down society. "Kit used to brief us before we went into interviews about what to say; sometimes to be as objectionable, arrogant and nasty as possible," Townshend later told the newspaper the *Observer*.[6]

The Who needed a song to match their abrasive reputation, and in October 1965 they started working on "My Generation." "I hope I die before I get old," sang Daltrey. Unlike their parents, this generation wanted to burn out early and not

Queen of the Mods

Cathy McGowan was hired as a producer and host of *Ready Steady Go!* when she was only 19 years old. She made the show a success because she was around the same age as the viewers and introduced them to trending fashions. Girls wanted to be like McGowan, and they tuned into *Ready Steady Go!* to see what she wore.

The Who's appearances on *Ready Steady Go!* helped them connect to a wider audience.

work themselves into the grave. "Why don't you all f-f-f-fade away," Daltrey stuttered, but crowds of mods improvised their own lyrics, and "f*** off" replaced "fade away."[7] The British Broadcasting Company (BBC) banned the song lest it offend anyone who stuttered.

DALTREY AXED

Success meant new problems. At one show, the enthusiastic crowd pulled Daltrey offstage, injuring his back. Then the van with the band's equipment was stolen. While the band was touring Denmark, the crowd stormed the stage and damaged the band's gear.

An increasingly serious problem was drug use. Moon, Townshend, and Entwistle all took amphetamines to keep up with the band's demanding schedule. In his memoir, *Thanks a Lot Mr Kibblewhite*, Daltrey admitted to trying purple hearts, an amphetamine, but they dried out his throat, and he couldn't sing. When the others performed high, they messed up the tempo and played so loudly that no one could hear Daltrey. After one particularly bad performance in 1965, Daltrey flushed Moon's stash down the toilet. When Daltrey admitted what he had done, Moon attacked him with a tambourine, and Daltrey punched Moon in the nose. The band fired Daltrey the next day.

Without Daltrey, crowds booed the Who off the stage. Lambert and Stamp asked him to return but said that if he hit someone again, he was gone. Daltrey stipulated that no one could perform stoned or use drugs while onstage because the music had to come first.

All the band members, including Daltrey, faced substance use problems during their careers.

This didn't stop the drinking or drug use entirely. Everyone in the band continued to drink, but none as much as Moon. In his memoir, Daltrey said Moon had vomit-inducing stage fright and started drinking to give himself the courage to go onstage. When the band wasn't on the road, Moon soon came to drink and take pills constantly, and Entwistle often partied with him. Prescription drugs were also a problem. Daltrey had trouble sleeping on the road, so his doctor prescribed sleeping pills. It took until 1973 for him to break the addiction. In the 1980s, Townshend's drinking forced him into rehab. As with many rock 'n' roll stars, substance abuse was a problem for the Who.

CHAPTER FOUR

Pop Art

As the Who came into their own, they left behind the understated mod style for the boldness of Pop art, which often incorporated black lines and bright blocks of color as well as images from advertising. One of the most well-known Pop art paintings is Andy Warhol's *Campbell's Soup Cans.* Townshend wore a khaki military-style shirt covered in World War I (1914–1918) medals he found in the antique shop his parents owned. He also put the Royal Air Force symbol, a target-like circle with a blue outer ring and red center, on a T-shirt. Moon wore T-shirts with targets, the word "Pow!," or sayings like "Elvis for Everyone." The shirts

The band members took on Pop art styles in their fashion and music as their careers progressed.

were adapted from Jasper Johns and Peter Blake's Pop art paintings of targets. Entwistle's jacket had military insignia such as stripes or chevrons on the sleeves. These clothes were entirely different from mod fashions, but they were still antiestablishment because none of the band members had served in the military, yet they coopted these symbols of military rank and honor.

It isn't surprising that Townshend, still at Ealing Art College, led the foray into Pop art. He combined things he heard at school with ideas from fans to create the band's new look. Pop art as a movement grew from the 1950s into the 1960s, because young artists felt that what they learned in art school or saw in museums had nothing to do with the world they lived in. They turned to popular culture to represent their reality, taking inspiration from everyday things like product

Union Jack

Photographs of the Who show both Entwistle and Townshend wearing jackets made from the British flag, often called the Union Jack. Many people today who buy similar jackets see wearing them as an act of patriotism or even a tribute to the Who and other favorite rockers who wear clothing embellished with either the British or American flags. When the Who did it, it wasn't meant to be patriotic but to offend, much in the way Townshend and Entwistle wore military medals and insignia they hadn't earned.

packaging, advertising, movies, comic books, and music. British Pop art often comically exaggerated a feature of its subjects. This was reflected onstage when Townshend wore so many medals on his shirt that they got in the way when he windmilled. The look was outrageous and offensive to the older generation who had served in World War II—and the Who's fans loved it.

"SUBSTITUTE"

By now the Who appeared regularly on *Ready Steady Go!* and had a solid hit with "My Generation." They also toured, sometimes playing as many as three shows a night, yet they were barely getting by. Part of the problem was the deal they had signed with Talmy and the amount of profit that belonged to him. The relationship went from bad to worse in 1966 when Talmy wanted to release the song "Circles," but the band chose "Substitute" instead.

The band members wanted more say in what they recorded, so they left Talmy's label and recorded "Substitute" with Reaction, Robert Stigwood's record label. As sung by Daltrey, "Substitute" is menacing, and the lyrics spin an unfocused story about someone who is not as he seems. The flip side was a song called "Instant Party."

Townshend's windmill technique became a signature part of his guitar-playing style.

Talmy got a court order to block the record's release, claiming he owned "Instant Party." He succeeded because "Instant Party" was obviously modified from "Circles," which the band had recorded in his studio. The band released "Substitute" after recording a new, all-instrumental flip side, "Waltz for a Pig." "Substitute" remains popular more than 50 years after it was recorded.

To complete the break with Talmy and keep him from again filing suit, Stamp and Lambert made a deal. They promised him part of the income on all songs recorded by the band for the next five years. Freedom came with a price, but the band no longer had to work with Talmy.

B-Side Protest

"Waltz for a Pig," the B-side released with "Substitute," was an instrumental number recorded by the Who Orchestra. The Who Orchestra was actually the Graham Bond Organisation, a British R&B group that included Graham Bond, who sang and played alto sax, saxophonist Dick Heckstall-Smith, and drummer Ginger Baker. Music industry insiders say the track mocks Talmy, which may be why Baker didn't initially take credit for writing it. On the record label, it is credited to Harry Butcher, a nod to the nursery rhyme "Rub-a-Dub-Dub," which includes the line "the butcher, the baker, the candlestick maker."

THE AMERICAN INVASION

To become a major rock band, the Who had to break into the larger US market. This meant the managers needed to sign the group with a booking agent, someone who could plan their US tour. Lambert and Stamp's first choice was Premier Talent, run by chief executive officer (CEO) Frank Barsalona and his partner Dick Friedberg, but Barsalona disliked the Who and refused to sign them. When Stamp discovered Barsalona was on a long trip, he flew to the United States and met with Friedberg. By the time Barsalona returned, Stamp was back in the United Kingdom, and the Who had a contract signed by Friedberg.

> "Although we didn't think it was such a bad deal at the time, we then learned about other deals."[1]
>
> *– Chris Stamp talking about the deal he and Kit Lambert made between the Who and Shel Talmy*

In 1967, the Who made their US debut, stopping first in New York City. Ending the show by smashing their equipment, they were unlike any other band US music lovers had ever seen. By the end of the seven-day tour, the Who had destroyed 22 microphones, four speaker cabinets, five guitars, and a ten-piece drum kit.

The Who next returned to the United States because they had been invited to play at the Monterey International Pop Festival on June 17 in

Monterey, California. The festival featured major talent, including rock acts Janis Joplin, Jefferson Airplane, and Jimi Hendrix.

Townshend and Entwistle later complained that their sound at Monterey was wrong because they had to use borrowed amps. Even so, the band stunned the crowd with its massive sound and the explosive ending to "My Generation" when smoke bombs triggered onstage. This performance catapulted them to US fame.

The Who and the Vietnam War

When the Who first made it to the United States, the Vietnam War (1954–1975) was in full swing, with President Lyndon Johnson sending more troops to fight in Vietnam. Musicmakers weren't just providing the soundtrack for protests against the war. They were also seen as instigators, commenting on society, the war, and politics. Music was a big part of Americans' Vietnam War protest movement. To the Who, the Vietnam War and the damage it caused looked a lot like what their parents had come through and what Britain was still recovering from.

Following this high, they returned home to troubling news. The Rolling Stones' Mick Jagger and Keith Richards had been tried for drug-related offenses, and both were found guilty. With public protests and their lawyers' appeal of the charges, they spent less than two days in prison—but both had been convicted. The news was a stark warning

The Who's performance at the Monterey International Pop Festival helped raise the band's profile internationally.

for rock bands whose members used drugs, including the Who. Such convictions could make getting the necessary paperwork to tour in certain countries impossible.

THE WHO SELL OUT

The Who were serious about their music and being countercultural, but they weren't beyond making fun of themselves. Their next album was *The Who Sell Out*, a Pop art celebration of consumption.

They marketed the album with a series of fake advertisements in which Townshend used an enormous deodorant, Moon daubed on medication from a giant tube of acne cream, and Daltrey sat in a bathtub full of Heinz baked beans. Like Pop artists, Townshend had mixed feelings toward commercialism. Like Pop art, rock music was both art and something to be sold and consumed, like a can of baked beans.

The record included "I Can See for Miles," a song Townshend had held back for a year, waiting for the right moment. This song made it to Number 10 on the US charts, which was an excellent showing given that no one in the United States had known who the band was six months earlier. But it only made it to Number 9 on the British charts. The band was going to have to do something bigger to make it to the very top.

CHAPTER FIVE

Success

By 1969, money was coming in reliably. Endless touring was no longer essential, and the band members' lives began to change. Townshend married his girlfriend, Karen Astley, and together they moved into a large West London property. Moon and his wife, Kim, moved to Highgate village near London with their daughter Mandy. Village life bored Moon, however, and he often went into West London to find alcohol and parties. Entwistle, like Moon, still gravitated toward the party scene, although he didn't lose control like the drummer, who had been nicknamed "Moon the Loon."

The members of the Who posed for cameras before going onstage for a show at the London Coliseum in February 1969.

Perhaps the biggest change was seen in Daltrey. Now that he was no longer combative, the others teasingly called him "Peaceful Perce" after his working-class childhood home on Percy Road. Daltrey credits his attitude change with no longer partying, which he formerly did after gigs, and focusing on life at the Berkshire County cottage he shared with his girlfriend, American model Heather Taylor.

To top it off, the band was getting along better than ever before. Daltrey believed that this was, in part, due to their US tour in June 1969. "I think America really brought us together. It was just the four of us and two tour managers, so we had to come together 'cos there was nobody else," Daltrey said.[1] The band was in San Francisco, California, when it learned Jann Wenner, the publisher of *Rolling Stone* magazine, who had once called the band almost too English, had nominated it for *Rolling Stone*'s Band of the Year.

TOMMY

Townshend came to understand that, just as Pop art was true art, pop music was not a short-lived fad and could be true art as well. With this in mind, he played with the idea of an album that told a story, a rock-and-roll opera. His idea was similar to recent albums such as the Beatles' *Sgt. Pepper's Lonely*

Hearts Club Band that were arranged around a specific theme.

Townshend's original idea for this album, first called *The Amazing Journey*, was about a boy who was born unable to see, hear, or speak but lived a rich life in his imagination and received sensory input only through vibration. As the album was recorded, the character shifted. The boy, Tommy, is born able to see, hear, and speak, but he withdraws when he witnesses his parents commit a murder and is repeatedly told to keep quiet. In Townshend's original idea, Tommy is again drawn out into the world by rock and roll, but music columnist Nik Cohn told Townshend that this idea would only earn *Tommy* four out of five stars in a review. Because Cohn was a pinball fan, Townshend suggested

Theme Albums

In 1967, a new type of rock album came into vogue. Instead of simply including enough songs to fill time on a record, a theme album's songs had a shared theme and were meant to be listened to in the order they appeared on the album. The first and most well-known album of this kind was the Beatles' *Sgt. Pepper's Lonely Hearts Club Band*, but other albums include the Kinks' *The Kinks Are The Village Green Preservation Society*, the Small Faces' *Ogdens' Nut Gone Flake*, and *S. F. Sorrow* by the Pretty Things. Though each was united by a common theme, there was no continuous plot or character interaction used to create a story such as Townshend developed in *Tommy*.

Townshend at work in his home studio in 1969

pinball as the solution, and Cohn agreed that was a five-star idea. This led to the popular, upbeat song "Pinball Wizard."

Fans often give Townshend full credit for the album, called *Tommy*, but it was a true collaboration. Entwistle wrote two songs, "Cousin Kevin," which is about bullying, and "Fiddle About," in which Tommy is molested by an uncle. Moon suggested that they set part of the story at a seaside camp like those visited by many British

families, including Townshend's. When it came time to record, Daltrey asked to sing the part of Tommy on the album and submerged himself in the songs, discussing the nuances with his bandmates. *Tommy*, more than any other Who album, was a group project.

Tommy was released in May 1969. Although the album was well received, it was in concert that it had its greatest impact. With the *Tommy* tour, Who concerts doubled in length. Their playing

"It was at the time very un-Wholike. A lot of the songs were sort of soft. We never played like that."[2]

– *Moon on the album* Tommy

was tighter and disciplined, and their concerts were critically acclaimed. This band's widening appeal was reflected in the venues where it performed *Tommy*, which included concert halls and opera houses that typically featured only classical music.

WOODSTOCK

In part because of *Tommy*'s success, the Who were invited to Woodstock. This legendary music festival took place from August 15 to 18, 1969, on a dairy farm in Bethel, New York. Half a million people attended, and performers included Jefferson Airplane, Jimi Hendrix, the Grateful Dead, and Janis Joplin. Festivalgoers camped and slept out on the grass, and despite rainy weather, everyone felt a pervasive harmony. "That's what means the

"See Me, Feel Me"

"See Me, Feel Me" is the last song on the album *Tommy*. In this song, Tommy, who can now see, hear, and speak, marvels at the world and future experiences spread out before him. With lyrics like "Listening to you, I get the music," it was the perfect song to end a set at a festival like Woodstock that was focused on hope and new experiences.

most to me—the connection to one another felt by all of us who worked on the festival, all those who came to it, and the millions who couldn't be there but were touched by it," said Michael Lang, one of the four concert organizers.[3]

The band didn't go onstage until sometime after 5:00 a.m. on August 17. Daltrey didn't feel like the performance was going well. Equipment malfunctioned in the damp, the sound was bad, and everyone was having trouble keeping focused because they were exhausted. Meanwhile, the Who's tight, aggressive performance contrasted with the laid-back, drugged euphoria of many of the acts and of the crowd.

Hippie Vibe

Among the fans at Woodstock were hippies, members of another counterculture movement. They stood against the materialism and repressive aspects of the dominant culture in the United States. Many of the men wore beards, and men and women dressed in brightly colored tie-dyed clothing with sandals and beads. A popular saying among hippies was "make love, not war." They promoted an open lifestyle including drug use, especially marijuana and LSD, and open sexual relationships. LSD is a drug that causes users to have strong hallucinations. Although many rock bands are considered countercultural, the Who were not hippies. Townshend in particular was suspicious of the movement and disliked LSD when he tried it.

The Woodstock festival attracted a vast number of music fans to rural New York.

Just after 6:00 a.m., though, something extraordinary happened. As they started to play a song from *Tommy*, "See Me, Feel Me," the sun came over the horizon. The song is about being able to see new possibilities in the world, so the

timing felt otherworldly. "It was one of those moments you couldn't ever re-create if you tried. Once in a lifetime," wrote Daltrey.[4] After performing at Woodstock, the Who became superstars.

CHAPTER SIX

The Stress of Success

After *Tommy*'s wild popularity, the Who felt pressured to once again achieve a similar level of success. It was a stressful time made even more so by a tragedy in Moon's life. He had agreed to speak at the opening of a new disco in Hertfordshire, north of London. When his group arrived on January 4, 1970, Moon focused on his fans, but even during his speech there was tension. A group of skinheads, an aggressive punk subculture, was intent on causing trouble, so Moon's group returned to their car. When some skinheads threw stones at the car, Moon's friend and driver Neil Boland got out to confront them but was

A tragedy involving Keith Moon in early 1970 took a heavy toll on the drummer.

surrounded. Moon panicked and, in trying to drive away, struck and killed Boland. The court ruled it an accident, but Moon, who had been drinking, blamed himself. Entwistle visited his friend, but Moon sank into depression.

Meanwhile, Townshend was trying to determine how best to create a live album. He wanted to give fans the band's energy, vitality, and even its rage from concerts in a package they could take home. To create a live album, the best songs from a number of shows are selected, combining popular songs with newer numbers. But instead of using songs recorded on the band's recent American tour, Townshend insisted upon using new material.

Fortunately, the Who had gigs scheduled at Leeds and Hull in England. These shows were recorded on February 14 and 15, 1970, but in Hull something had not been set up correctly,

Burned

The Who could have used recordings from a recent tour to compile a live album. They had done 30 shows in the United States and eight in Britain. But Townshend realized that going through those recordings just one time would take eight long days in the studio. Choosing the tracks for a live album would require listening to tapes multiple times, and the task seemed overwhelming. With his usual dramatic flair, Townshend ordered the recordings burned. The only way to make a live album would be to make new recordings.

and Entwistle's bass could not be heard on several tracks. The band had to rely on the Leeds recordings to assemble the album. *Live at Leeds*, released in May 1970, was honest and raw because it captured a single concert. There were no retakes and no second chances. Critics loved the album, with the *New York Times* calling it "the best live rock album ever made" and Jonathan Eisen of *Circus* magazine saying that the album was inspired in how it harnessed the Who's energy.[1]

Quiet Creativity

The album cover for *Live at Leeds* may look casual, but a lot of effort went into creating its look. The cover was brown cardboard with "The Who Live at Leeds" in block letters that appeared to have been hand stamped. The sleeve had two pockets, one of which held the actual record. The second held copies of a variety of memorabilia including a photo of the band, handwritten lyrics from the chorus of "Listening to You" from *Tommy*, and a reproduction of a 1964 classic black-and-white poster with Townshend windmilling.

LIFEHOUSE

Even with the success of *Live at Leeds*, the pressure was still on for a hit to rival *Tommy*. In August 1970, Townshend started writing "The Pete Townshend Page" in *Melody Maker*, the largest weekly music publication in Britain. In this column, Townshend worked through the ideas that became *Lifehouse*.

Live at Leeds managed to capture the unique energy and atmosphere of a Who live performance.

> "It might have helped if we'd taken the idea into the studio to knock it about. . . . He took all the pressure of coming up with next big thing on his own."[2]
>
> *– Daltrey on Townshend's struggle to develop* Lifehouse*, 2018*

Set in a future without rock and roll, *Lifehouse* tells the story of a polluted world where people must wear life suits that give them nutrients and sensory input. Bobby, a young electronics genius, discovers that exposure to music can help people attain enlightenment, removing them from government control. Among the new songs Townshend wrote for *Lifehouse* were "Baba O'Reilly," about trying to find the way through a "teenage wasteland," and "Won't Get Fooled Again," about a revolution that fails because the new leadership is the same as the old. Townshend believed *Lifehouse* could change society, but because he knew the message was so important, he felt immense pressure to get everything right. It didn't help that Townshend's vision required inventing new technologies so he could record the music on four channels versus the two used in stereo recordings. Problems mounted and Townshend gave up in the midst of his first nervous breakdown.

Though *Lifehouse* was abandoned, songs from the project were compiled into the album

Nervous Breakdown

Stress over *Lifehouse* caused Townshend to suffer a nervous breakdown. *Nervous breakdown* is not a medical term and doesn't identify a specific problem. In the past, it was used to describe when someone became so stressed that they could not cope with the demands placed on them. It also can be used to describe situations brought on by depression and anxiety, both diagnosable disorders. Possible symptoms that would lead to this description included the inability to work, problems sleeping or eating, change in hygiene, and avoiding people.

Who's Next, which was released in 1971. Former *Lifehouse* tracks included "Baba O'Riley" and "Won't Get Fooled Again." The album is often considered the band's best, showcasing Townshend's writing ability and Daltrey's voice to their utmost. Reviewers noted that the organ in "Baba O'Riley" didn't just provide sounds but also the rhythm of the song, much as Townshend played the rhythm on his guitar. In *Sounds* newspaper, Bill Walker said of this album, "After the unique brilliance of *Tommy* something special had to be thought out and the fact that they settled for a straightforward album rather than a rock opera, says much for their courage and inventiveness."[3]

QUADROPHENIA

In August 1972, Townshend told *Sounds* that he was working on another rock opera. Early on

Townshend saw it as a story of a character, Jimmy, with a four-way personality split. Each aspect of his personality represented one member of the Who. Townshend said people take advantage of Jimmy because he is sometimes an underachiever. This aspect of the character represented Townshend. As a thug capable of stealing or smashing up someone's home, he was Daltrey, the romantic aspect was Entwistle, and the dangerously out-of-control aspect was Moon. Townshend later admitted that the four personality aspects and how each represented a band member were not a large part of the new album. He had emphasized it in interviews to draw US fans to the album.

Lifehouse as a Graphic Novel

A graphic novel of *Lifehouse* was scheduled for release in 2020 by the science fiction magazine *Heavy Metal.* The adaptation was written and illustrated by James Harvey, the author-illustrator of the book *Mouth Baby.* "Harvey's storytelling, an infusion of graphic design, mod and Japanese styles, exactly fit what we were looking for," said *Heavy Metal* CEO Jeff Krelitz.[4] The project was undertaken because the dystopian themes of *Lifehouse* feel relevant today, alongside modern themes of politics, dependence on technology, and global warming.

The album is about the early mods and their fights with rockers. The central character, Jimmy, slaves away at a job he hates when he would

John Entwistle onstage during the supporting tour for *Quadrophenia*

rather be taking drugs, having sex, or getting in a fight. Eventually his parents throw him out, his friends abandon him, and his scooter is destroyed in an accident. Jimmy returns to Brighton where, in the midst of chaos, he last felt alive. There he sees a mod face he used to look up to in a menial, service job. His mod ideals have let him down, and the album ends with him on a seaside cliff contemplating his life. The listener must decide what happens next.

Released in October 1973, *Quadrophenia* was hailed as a masterpiece. Chris Welch, writing in *Melody Maker*, gushed about the album, calling it a "battle cry and a hammer of heartbeats." Where *Tommy* was abstract, *Quadrophenia* was just the opposite. Said Welch, "*Quadrophenia*, though it deals in aggression, frustration, and sorrows, is so real you can almost taste the HP Sauce and smell the [cigarette] ash."[5] The album reached Number 2 in the United States and in Britain.

CHAPTER SEVEN

The Big Screen

The Who still needed a hit to rival *Tommy.* Their next opportunity would be the film version of *Tommy* directed by Ken Russell. He had done movies about composers, including *The Dance of the Seven Veils* (1970) about Richard Strauss and *The Music Lovers* (1970) about Pyotr Ilyich Tchaikovsky. Like the Who, Russell was seen as wild and subversive, yet his films were successful. *Tommy* the movie was released on March 26, 1975. The album provides the soundtrack in its entirety. In addition to providing the music, the characters speak only through the songs as in traditional opera.

Daltrey starred in the title role in the film adaptation of *Tommy.*

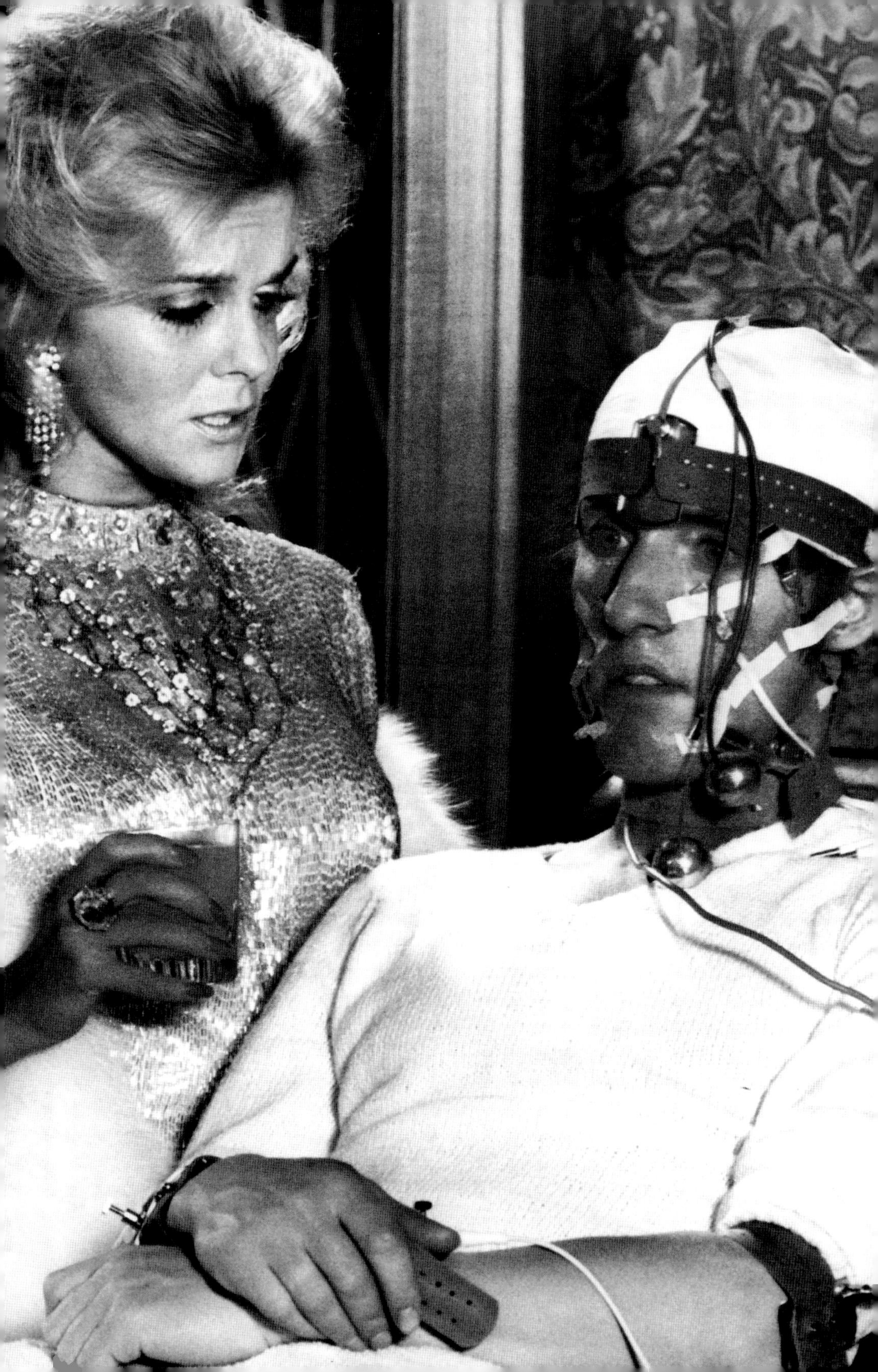

The film was definitely subversive, with Tommy's stepfather taking him to the Acid Queen, played by famous American soul singer Tina Turner. Many people believed this character represented drug use. Townshend explained she was a metaphor for peer pressure, promising to cure him through drug use while actually using drugs to destroy him. The movie often comes across as a prolonged acid trip with bizarre imagery like Tommy's mother, played by actress Ann-Margret, writhing in baked beans. Still the overall feel of the movie fit in well with British cinema of the day—peculiar and cheeky, according to Who biographer Ben Marshall. But Russell's *Tommy* diverged in so many ways from Townshend's original vision that sometimes Russell also subverted Townshend's message, focusing on bizarre imagery and excess versus Townshend's explorations of reality.

Despite these differences from the

Uncomfortable Front Man

Daltrey may have been the front man for the Who, but the movie catapulted him out of his comfort zone. At one public appearance, thousands of fans showed up. Daltrey felt like they wanted to see Tommy the character and not Daltrey the singer. Daltrey also appeared on American talk shows, which his accent made problematic. "They couldn't understand me. Culturally as well as literally," said Daltrey.[1] To make it all the more embarrassing, when he got really stressed, he stuttered.

album, the film grabbed people's attention. The world depicted in the film was one of unthinking excess, much the way people thought of the rock world. People who would never have gone to a Who concert went to see the movie, and they liked what they saw. Daltrey played Tommy in the film, and his straight mod hair had been replaced with his natural curls. He spends much of the movie staring wide-eyed into the distance. Tommy somehow remained untouched by the corruption around him. Daltrey became a star.

Awards for *Tommy*

Fans are often surprised that the movie *Tommy* didn't win more awards than it did. In 1975, at the first annual Rock Music Awards, *Tommy* won Best Rock Movie or Theatrical Production. At the 1976 Academy Awards in the United States, Swedish-American actress Ann-Margret was nominated for best actress for her part as Tommy's mother, and Pete Townshend was nominated for Best Music. At the 1976 Golden Globes, an American award given by the Hollywood Foreign Press Association for excellence in television and film, Ann-Margret won best actress. The film was nominated for Best Motion Picture—Music or Comedy, and Roger Daltrey was nominated for Best Acting Debut, but these awards went to other nominees.

PUNK ROCK VERSUS ROCK AND ROLL

In the 1960s, mods had looked at the frugality of their parents and demanded something different. They were tired of the day-to-day struggle to get by. They wanted to live the high life, listening to loud music and partying, complete with alcohol, amphetamines, and sex.

In the mid-1970s, punk rockers looked around and saw established people with power and money on the one hand and people struggling to get by on the other hand. It was easy for the punk musicians, like the Sex Pistols, to identify themselves as "have nots" and call established rockers, like the Rolling Stones and David Bowie, the "haves."

Established rock musicians had every reason to be worried because they hadn't just made their way into modern music. They had essentially wiped their predecessors out of existence. Rock bands had taken over the clubs and popular music. But now that they had succeeded, according to punk rockers, they weren't revolutionaries anymore. Even when the Who made *The*

The Loudest Band on Earth

In 1976, the Who played a concert tour, The Who Put the Boot In, as a series of events at soccer stadiums. These venues were significantly larger than their usual venues and allowed more fans to buy tickets. At the May 31 concert at the Charlton Athletic Grounds, the band set a new world record, but it wasn't for attendance. *The Guinness Book of World Records* measured the volume at 120 decibels.[2] This is nearly the sound level of a jet engine, making the Who the loudest band ever.

Guinness Book of World Records as the loudest band, they were still the establishment—moneyed, settled, and even friendly with the British royal family. Established rock bands worried that the punk bands would wipe them out as they had their predecessors.

The members of the Who could have made easy targets. Yet punk rockers favored the Who. One evening in January 1977, Townshend encountered Paul Cook, the Sex Pistols' drummer, and Steve Jones, the group's guitarist, in the Speakeasy, an after-hours club. There Townshend discovered that Cook and Jones admired the Who. However, Townshend was disappointed that they seemed interested only in being in a band and making money, not in making great music.

> "I felt I was spending all my time behind a desk and the Sex Pistols were out enjoying the dream."[3]
>
> *– Pete Townshend on the rise of punk rock, 1977*

WHO ARE YOU?

Toward the end of 1977, director Jeff Stein began work on *The Kids Are Alright*, a film history of the Who. He planned to use a lot of older footage, but he wanted new film as well. Two concerts were arranged, but he decided not to use anything from

To some people, it seemed as though punk rockers like the Sex Pistols would replace groups like the Who as countercultural icons.

the first event in December 1977. The band had not performed together in a year, and it showed. A May 1978 event proved better for Stein's purposes, but

it turned out to be significant for another reason. It would be the last concert Keith Moon played with the band.

Moon appeared at a film premiere in London the night before his death.

In 1978, the Who were recording their first album in three years. They desperately wanted it to be something that could compete with *Tommy*'s success, especially since the older album was selling better than ever because of the movie. But the project was proving difficult. Entwistle was mixing the soundtrack for *The Kids Are Alright*, which took hours of work. When they managed to get together to record, Moon had trouble keeping time on some days and on others he couldn't drum at all. As Daltrey later explained, Moon's drug and alcohol use had dramatically increased, resulting in five years of serious abuse. His body was worn out, and because he was a very physical drummer, drumming was always difficult and sometimes completely impossible.

Moon wasn't the only one having problems. Townshend had injured himself, putting his hand through a plate glass window. Daltrey had just had throat surgery to repair damage caused by an earlier throat infection. But Moon the Loon was the easiest scapegoat, and Townshend threatened to fire him. Despite the difficulties the band was having, it finished recording the album.

The new album, *Who Are You*, was released on August 18, 1978. Many of the tracks included prominent use of a synthesizer and lyrics about music as a metaphor for life, holdovers from

The Kids Are Alright

The documentary *The Kids Are Alright* was released in June 1979. Later, in 1996, Entwistle told *Goldmine* magazine that the producer added footage of Moon to the movie after the drummer's death. Every time Entwistle objected, saying it was exploitive, Stein cut one of Entwistle's scenes. "I figured, God, I'm not going to be in the movie if I argue anymore," Entwistle said.[4] The new scenes showed Moon at his worst and Entwistle didn't like the thought of people's last idea of Moon being negative.

Lifehouse. The album flew up the charts, landing at Number 2 in the United States and Canada and Number 6 in Great Britain.

But the band didn't get to celebrate this latest success. On September 7, 1978, Moon was found dead. He had died in his sleep. Although he had spent years ingesting huge amounts of alcohol and pills, he had been in the process of getting his life together. He died of a massive overdose of Heminevrin, a prescription he had been given by his doctor to help him stop drinking alcohol. Moon had taken many more pills at one time than the doctor prescribed. As explained by a biographer, Tony Fletcher, Moon understood that alcohol and cocaine could kill, but

> "I think someone looked down and said, 'Okay, that's your ninth life.'"[5]
>
> *– John Entwistle on the death of Keith Moon, 1978*

Daltrey, *right*, at Moon's funeral, along with the Rolling Stones' Bill Wyman, *center*

he never made the same connection to anything prescribed by a doctor.

CHAPTER EIGHT

Quadrophenia Saves the Day

The time immediately after Keith Moon's death was tough for the bandmates. Work had begun on the film adaptation of the album *Quadrophenia*, and they almost called it off. Franc Roddam, the film's director, said producer Roy Baird and Bill Curbishley, the Who's manager at that time, kept the project on course. For Curbishley, a former mod, the project was personal, often feeling to him like a film of what he and fellow mods had gone through on the Brighton beach when fighting the rockers.

Released in 1979, *Quadrophenia* as a film was a much tighter story than the album. In it, Jimmy is a mod teen with a little money

The film adaptation of *Quadrophenia* depicted the 1964 brawl that had played a significant role in mod history.

Palace

One Director

As Franc Roddam was beginning to work on *Quadrophenia*, he received a visit from Townshend. The guitarist told Roddam how he wanted to do the music, but Roddam disagreed and explained to Townshend that he didn't see *Quadrophenia* as another rock opera. Instead he planned to make a movie about how life was for the mods. Roddam explained he would include a variety of rock and roll. Townshend ultimately went along with this idea. "He said I think you have a great approach to this thing, and if that's what you want to do, do it, and he stepped back," said Roddam of Townshend.[1]

who wants to be free of his parents' conservatism and thrift. He and his friends party and have sex and get into fights with rockers, but in the end, he discovers that his fellow mods aren't there for him any more than his parents are. The film is full of 1960s mod music, including "Zoot Suit" by the High Numbers and "Green Onions" by Booker T and the MG's.

The turmoil in the film spoke to British viewers in the 1970s. In Britain this was a time of strife stemming from several things, including a global energy crisis that was contributing to higher fuel costs. As prices soared, miners and other workers held strikes, demanding higher wages. The film was an overwhelming success in Britain perhaps in part because a mod resurgence was underway. Although these younger mods had their own bands, including the Jam, they often cited the Who as their inspiration.

In the United States, *Quadrophenia* had much less appeal. Americans didn't see themselves in how people in England once lived, and they didn't understand the beach riots. The film featured the music of the Who, but it was not in a package Americans easily understood.

The Mod Revival

A mod revival had already been going on prior to the release of *Quadrophenia*. It was fueled by the music of new mod bands, including not only the Jam but also the Lambrettas, the Purple Hearts, and the Merton Parkas. From 1978 to 1981, there were clashes between various youth subcultures—punks, mods, rockers, teddy boys, and skinheads. *Quadrophenia* the film fueled these clashes, which is ironic because it is a movie about the futility of these subcultures and how they will eventually fail to deliver the radical change participants seek.

THE WHO 2.0

To continue as a rock band, the Who would have to rely on studio drummers or hire a new drummer. Entwistle understood that replacing Moon would be impossible. "We'd need two drummers to replace him," he said.[2] On the other hand, Townshend and Daltrey both saw replacing Moon as an opportunity to reinvent the Who. "We can do anything we want to do now," Daltrey told Dave Marsh from *Rolling Stone* magazine, despite his sorrow at the loss of his friend.[3]

Townshend wanted to hire long-time friend Kenney Jones, drummer for the Small Faces, a mod band later known as the Faces. Moon had been a drummer who made things up as he went along, experimenting and ignoring the rules. Jones kept solid, tight time, a fact that Townshend in particular welcomed, feeling this would give him greater room to experiment.

Jones was later inducted into the Rock & Roll Hall of Fame, so he was clearly an excellent drummer, but Daltrey questioned whether Jones was the right choice. As he tells it in his memoir, he said Jones was the wrong drummer for the Who just as Moon would have been the wrong drummer for the Faces. But Townshend prevailed. Jones was made a full member of the band.

The Rock & Roll Hall of Fame

The Rock & Roll Hall of Fame is the world's largest museum devoted exclusively to rock and roll, its history, and its legacy. The Who were inducted into the Hall of Fame in 1990 with the original lineup including Keith Moon. Kenney Jones was honored in 2012 when the band the Small Faces/Faces was inducted. Like the Who, the Small Faces formed in 1965. In 1969, with a new lead singer and guitarist, they changed their name to Faces.

STRESSED TO BREAKING

Unfortunately, the band soon faced another tragedy. On December 3, 1979, they played a concert in Cincinnati, Ohio. Over

18,000 tickets, the majority as festival seating, had been sold. Festival seating isn't a ticket for a specific seat, but entrance into the venue. Because of this, thousands of fans who wanted to be sure they got good seats showed up hours before the doors opened.

> "There was nobody else, in my opinion."[6]
>
> *– Townshend on the Who's decision to hire Kenney Jones*

When they heard the band's sound check at 6:30 p.m., they pushed forward. It only got worse when the doors were eventually opened. People were pushed to the ground, where some were trampled. Other people never fell but were crushed, unable to breathe. Concertgoers reported that only two to four doors were open, though officials later claimed all 16 doors into the stadium were open. A total of 11 people died.[4] The band didn't find out until after the concert. This horrible news on top of exhaustion was just too much, and Daltrey remembers being numb.

Post-Moon, post-Cincinnati, the band recorded the album *It's Hard*, which was released in 1982. Despite the fact that Parke Puterbaugh of *Rolling Stone* magazine called it "their most vital and coherent album since *Who's Next*," Daltrey says that even while they were recording, something felt off.[5] Perhaps it was the new drummer, but the

A security guard studies the aftermath of the deadly stampede at the Cincinnati concert.

sound was simply not the Who. Some critics even said the band members were too old to be taken seriously. On December 16, 1983, Townshend announced at a press conference that he was leaving the band. The Who were at best on hiatus, at worst a thing of the past.

It's Hard

The reasons behind the failure of *It's Hard* were more complex than the addition of a new drummer. At the time the album was released, Townshend gave a number of candid interviews during which he admitted to extensive alcohol and heroin addiction, which had ruined his marriage. He also said that he had been through rehab and recovered, but drug use may also have impaired his ability to write new material. Townshend was also keeping his best material for his solo work. For years he felt as though he were giving everything to the band even though he'd also been creating solo albums. When they were creating *It's Hard*, he decided to save ten of the songs he'd written for himself.

CHAPTER NINE

Getting the Band Back Together

After the official breakup, the former members of the Who engaged in a variety of creative endeavors. In January 1984, Entwistle was part of a BBC television program in which he gave advice about playing the bass to new musicians. In August, he joined American rocker Bruce Springsteen onstage in Rutherford, New Jersey, to play the Isley Brothers' song "Twist and Shout."

Pete Townshend and his brother Simon Townshend worked on an album. Townshend also wrote several songs that appeared on later solo albums, including 1985's *White City*. In October, he held a concert to raise

Daltrey and the other members of the band worked individually following their breakup, but it would not be long before they collaborated again as the Who.

money to battle heroin addiction, performing at the event in Hampstead, England.

On February 17, 1984, Daltrey's solo album *Parting Should Be Painless* was released in Britain. Stylistically, it was more New Wave than rock, and critics called it disappointing. Colin Irwin in *Melody Maker* said the album had the "zest of a caterpillar."[1] In March, the album was released in the United States, and one critic, Wayne King in *Record,* questioned whether Daltrey really wanted a solo career.

The first time the Who played together again was in 1985 at Live Aid. The concert was a fundraiser to raise money to aid victims of famine in Africa. The concert took place on July 13 at Wembley Stadium in London and was organized by Bob Geldof, the singer in the Irish band Boomtown Rats. Once again the Who were at the right place because Live Aid was one of the biggest events in music history. Most of the over 75 acts performed at either Wembley or at JFK Stadium in Philadelphia, Pennsylvania. Satellites transmitted the event to one billion viewers in 110 nations.[2]

Joan Baez kicked off the performance in Philadelphia by telling fans that this was their Woodstock. Among the acts were Mick Jagger from the Rolling Stones, Run-DMC, David Bowie, and Sting. At Woodstock, the Who had wowed

the crowd, but at Live Aid their set went badly. In a 2015 article, the *New York Post* listed the Who as one of the five worst Live Aid performances. *Rolling Stone* magazine pointed out that the band clearly did not rehearse enough and thus was not well prepared, losing its way during the instrumental portion of "Won't Get Fooled Again." To make matters worse, the satellite cut out for most of two songs, leaving TV audiences in the dark, right after Daltrey sang the line "why don't you all just fade away" in "My Generation." Something was also wrong with Entwistle's bass, which cut out repeatedly. Still, the event generated $127 million to help famine victims and convinced various nations to supply grain to those in need.[3] After Live Aid, the members of the band went their separate ways.

HAPPY ANNIVERSARY

In 1989, Daltrey, Townshend, and Entwistle reunited for the Who's twenty-fifth anniversary tour, but they didn't try to replace Moon. Instead of playing with Jones, they used a variety of session singers and other musicians, including drummer Simon Phillips. He was trained in jazz, so he played with a looser style, changing up tempo and improvising. He was better able to emulate, if not replace, Moon.

The tour included performing *Tommy* in Los Angeles, New York, and London. Special celebrity guests took part in these performances, including Elton John, Steve Winwood, Billy Idol, Phil Collins, and Patti LaBelle. The tour was a huge success.

In the summer of 2002, Entwistle, Townshend, and Daltrey flew to the United States to start another major tour. One day before the tour was to begin, on June 27, 2002, Entwistle died in the Hard Rock Hotel and Casino in Las Vegas. The coroner said that he had had a heart attack caused by cocaine use.

It was decided that, as difficult as it would be, they would continue on the tour. British musician Pino Palladino replaced Entwistle on bass. Zak Starkey, the son of Beatles drummer Ringo Starr, played the drums, and Simon Townshend, Pete Townshend's younger brother, played a second

Hearing Damage

On their twenty-fifth anniversary tour, the Who made a point to tone down the volume. Townshend suffered from a ringing in his ears called tinnitus. Tinnitus can be related to age, or it can be caused by damage done to the ear by loud noises such as rock music. Townshend noted that he had problems whenever he played too loudly or stressed himself out. Daltrey has advised fans to wear earplugs to rock concerts to protect their hearing. He, too, has hearing loss and said that Entwistle wore hearing aids before he died.

guitar. But Entwistle, Daltrey, and Townshend had gone to school together and known each other since they were children. For Daltrey and Townshend, going on without their friend was a painfully difficult decision.

Going On

When Entwistle died, Townshend and Daltrey could have canceled the tour. Townshend noted how shattered Daltrey was. "He was shaking. He couldn't even hold a cup of tea," said Townshend.[4] But ultimately the pair decided that they needed to go on. Daltrey clarified the message that they wanted to send to the world. "I felt we should go on to show people our age that we are in the drop zone," he said, referring to the fact that as people age, more and more of their friends and loved ones die from a variety of health problems. "What do you do when your mates die? You can't stop living. You've got to go on," Daltrey said.[5]

STILL MAKING MUSIC

Townshend and Daltrey continue to make music together as the Who. In 2014 and 2015, they toured Britain and the United States in The Who Hits 50, a tour to celebrate 50 years making music together. In interviews, the pair acknowledged how lucky they were to still be doing what they loved and sharing it with their fans.

Although the fiftieth-anniversary tour was called their final farewell to fans, Daltrey and Townshend took to

Daltrey and Townshend, who began performing together in the 1960s, continued to appear side by side onstage through the 2010s.

the road again in 2019. They had a new album to promote, their first in 13 years. *WHO* was released in the fall of 2019 and included only new songs, including "Ball and Chain," a swamp-rock critique of the US treatment of prisoners being detained in Guantánamo Bay, Cuba.

Unlike some of the Who's earlier albums, this one didn't have a theme. It wasn't a rock opera, and it didn't tell a story. The songs were written by Pete and Simon Townshend. Pete Townshend explained that the songs were composed to inspire Daltrey and show the range of his voice. That's quite a change from 1965, when Townshend referred to Moon and Entwistle as geniuses and Daltrey as "just a singer."[6] For his part, Daltrey said that he thinks the album is their best since *Quadrophenia*. "Pete hasn't lost it, he's still a fabulous songwriter and he's still got that cutting edge."[7]

Swamp Rock

"Ball and Chain," one of the songs on *WHO*, is in a musical style known as swamp rock. In many ways swamp rock is a nod back to the Who's roots. Skiffle was similar to rockabilly, and swamp rock draws on rockabilly as well as mid-1960s soul. Gritty and heavily rhythmic, one of the best-known swamp rock bands is Creedence Clearwater Revival. The sound is exemplified by their song "Born on the Bayou." Other swamp-rock songs include Tony Joe White's "Polk Salad Annie" and "Big Boss Man" by Elvis Presley.

It is this cutting-edge quality that drew fans to the Who in their original days as a mod band. That same energy propelled the Who through decades of success in rock and roll. Other artists, including Pearl Jam's Eddie Vedder, Billie Joe Armstrong of Green Day, and Bono from U2 were influenced by the Who. When rockers create fashion lines, the band's influence extends there as well. A green parka, much like the one worn by Jimmy in *Quadrophenia*, is part of the clothing line designed by Liam Gallagher of the British band Oasis. The impact of the Who continues because their music about the lives of young music fans, and the challenges those fans face, continues to resonate with music lovers and musicmakers.

> "Roger and I are both old men now, by any measure, so I've tried to stay away from romance, but also from nostalgia if I can. . . . Some of the songs refer to the explosive state of things today."[8]
>
> *– Townshend on their 2019 tour and the album* WHO, *2019*

TIMELINE

1944

Roger Daltrey is born on March 1 in West London; John Entwistle is born on October 9 in West London.

1945

Pete Townshend is born on May 19 in West London.

1946

Keith Moon is born on August 23 in northwestern London.

1961

Roger Daltrey forms the skiffle band the Detours.

1964

The Detours change their name to the Who and Keith Moon joins the band; on March 28 and March 29, fights between mods and rockers take place in Clacton, England, and more fights happen in Brighton on May 16–18; in September, Townshend smashes a guitar for the first time during a performance at the Railway Hotel and Club.

1967

The Who first tour the United States, performing in New York City. On June 17, they take part in the Monterey International Pop Festival in Monterey, California.

1969

The album *Tommy* is released in May; on August 17, the Who take part in Woodstock.

1970

On January 4, Keith Moon accidentally runs over and kills his friend and driver Neil Boland; in May, the album *Live at Leeds* is released.

1973

The album *Quadrophenia* is released in October.

1975

The movie *Tommy* is released in March.

1978

On September 7, Keith Moon dies from a drug overdose.

1979

The movie *Quadrophenia* is released.

1983

On December 16, Pete Townshend announces at a press conference that he is leaving the band.

1985

The Who reunite to play at Live Aid but are criticized for a poor performance.

2002

On June 27, John Entwistle dies of a heart attack brought on by cocaine use.

2019

The Who release the album *WHO*, featuring all-new material.

ESSENTIAL FACTS

The Who Band Members

- **Roger Daltrey** formed the band and sang lead beginning in 1961. He may be best known for playing Tommy in the movie of the same name.
- **John Entwistle** was the bass player from 1961 until his death in 2002. He was also a songwriter for the band.
- **Pete Townshend** played lead guitar beginning in 1962. He is the band's principal songwriter, although he sought input from his bandmates on projects, most notably *Tommy*.
- **Keith Moon** played the drums for the band from 1964 until his death in 1978. His unconventional, high-energy style assured that he was never in the background.

The Who Studio Albums

- *My Generation* (1965)
- *A Quick One* (1966)
- *The Who Sell Out* (1967)
- *Tommy* (1969)
- *Who's Next* (1971)
- *Quadrophenia* (1973)
- *The Who by Numbers* (1975)
- *Who Are You* (1978)
- *Face Dances* (1981)
- *It's Hard* (1982)
- *Endless Wire* (2006)
- *WHO* (2019)

Career Highlights

The Who are known both for their energetic stage presence and for their musical innovation. Guitarist Pete Townshend developed a lead guitar style that emphasized the song's rhythm. This left space for bass player John Entwistle to showcase his talent in bass solos. Drummer Keith Moon refused to remain in the background, the custom for drummers at that time, and played drum solos.

Their high-energy stage acts drew crowds, especially after 1964 when Townshend and Moon first destroyed their instruments at the end of the show. In part because of their stage presence, they were invited to both the 1967 Monterey Pop Festival and the Woodstock music festival in 1969. They also created one of the most innovative albums in the history of rock music with their 1969 rock opera *Tommy*. The band continues to make music, creating new songs after more than 50 years together.

Conflicts

Within the band, Daltrey and Moon had a particularly contentious relationship. When Daltrey flushed Moon's drug stash in 1965, Moon attacked Daltrey, and Daltrey punched him in the face, getting himself briefly thrown out of the band. Drug abuse and alcohol often fueled these disagreements.

Quote

"There were a few laughs. . . . Everyone was waiting for me to kind of sob over my guitar. . . . That'll teach you to be flash. . . . I had no recourse but to completely look as though I meant to do it, so I smashed the guitar and jumped all over the bits."

—Pete Townshend on the beginnings of his iconic onstage guitar smashing

GLOSSARY

album
A collection of songs published under a title.

amplifier
An electronic device used to increase the volume of a guitar or a singer's voice, called an amp for short.

bass guitar
A guitar instrument with a low tonal range.

counterculture
A culture of values that go against those of established society, popularized in the 1960s.

evacuate
To remove something from a particular place, often because of danger.

face
In mod slang, a person who wears the proper mod fashions and has the right taste in music.

flash
In mod slang, to show off or be conspicuous.

flip side
The less important side of a single record, also called the B side.

producer
A person who supervises or finances a work, such as a play, film, or recording, for exhibition to the public.

punk rock
A loud, aggressive type of rock popular in the late 1970s and early 1980s.

R&B
Rhythm and blues; a type of pop music of African American origin that has a soulful vocal style that features improvisation.

session musician
A musician hired to work in a recording session or performance rather than as a permanent member of a band.

single
A song or track released to the public independently, not as part of a complete album.

skiffle
A kind of folk music with a blues or jazz influence, played by a small group, that often used improvised musical instruments, such as washboards.

subculture
A small culture with interests and beliefs that are new or different from those of the larger culture or society.

zoot suit
A style of men's suit from the 1940s with a long, loose jacket with padded shoulders and high-waisted, narrow-legged trousers. It became popular among mods.

ADDITIONAL RESOURCES

Selected Bibliography

Daltrey, Roger. *Thanks a Lot Mr Kibblewhite: My Story*. Holt, 2018.

Fletcher, Tony. *Moon: The Life and Death of a Rock Legend*. Spike, 1999.

Marshall, Ben. *The Who: The Official History*. Harper Design, 2015.

Townshend, Pete. *Who I Am*. HarperCollins, 2015.

Further Readings

Dodge Cummings, Judy. *The Beatles*. Abdo, 2022.

Moore, Shannon Baker. *A History of Music*. Abdo, 2015.

Wheeler, Jill C. *The Rolling Stones*. Abdo, 2022.

Online Resources

To learn more about the Who, please visit **abdobooklinks.com** or scan this QR code. These links are routinely monitored and updated to provide the most current information available.

More Information

For more information on this subject, contact or visit the following organizations:

The Museum at Bethel Woods
200 Hurd Rd.
Bethel, NY 12720
845-583-2079
bethelwoodscenter.org/museum

The main exhibit at this museum is "Woodstock and the Sixties." Visit where the Woodstock music festival took place.

The Rock & Roll Hall of Fame
1100 Rock and Roll Blvd.
Cleveland, OH 44114
216-781-7625
rockhall.com

The Rock & Roll Hall of Fame commemorates critical contributions to rock and roll. Its museum chronicles the history of rock music, including artists, producers, and even sound engineers. The website includes information on inductees, including the artists they influenced and recordings of their songs.

SOURCE NOTES

CHAPTER 1. DESTRUCTION

1. "The Who." *Rock & Roll Hall of Fame*, n.d., rockhall.com. Accessed 29 Aug. 2019.
2. Marsh, Dave. *Before I Get Old.* New York: St. Martin's Press, 1983. 90.
3. Marsh, *Before I Get Old,* 123.
4. Marsh, *Before I Get Old,* 124.
5. Marsh, *Before I Get Old,* 125.
6. Marsh, *Before I Get Old,* 126.
7. Marsh, *Before I Get Old,* 122.

CHAPTER 2. THE BEGINNING

1. Terry Charman. "What Life Was Like in Britain During the Second World War." *Imperial War Museum*, 8 Jan. 2018, iwm.org.uk. Accessed 26 Sept. 2019.
2. "1921." *Genius*, n.d., genius.com. Accessed 26 Sept. 2019.
3. Ben Marshall. *The Who: The Official History.* Harper Design, 2015. 52.
4. Pete Townshend. *Who I Am: A Memoir.* Harper, 2012. 59.
5. Dave Marsh. *Before I Get Old.* St. Martin's Press, 1983. 65–66.

CHAPTER 3. THE MODS

1. Jon Savage. "Mods v Rockers: Two Tribes Go To War." *BBC*, 21 Oct. 2014, bbc.com. Accessed 28 Sept. 2019.
2. Savage, "Mods v Rockers: Two Tribes Go To War."
3. Savage, "Mods v Rockers: Two Tribes Go To War."
4. Savage, "Mods v Rockers: Two Tribes Go To War."
5. Andrew Loog Oldham. *Stoned: A Memoir of London in the 1960's.* Random House, 2010. 347.
6. Ben Marshall. *The Who: The Official History.* Harper Design, 2015. 89.
7. Marshall, *The Who: The Official History,* 93–94.

CHAPTER 4. POP ART

1. Dave Marsh. *Before I Get Old*. St. Martin's Press, 1983. 204.

CHAPTER 5. SUCCESS

1. Ben Marshall. *The Who: The Official History.* Harper Design, 2015. 150.

2. Tony Fletcher. *Moon: The Life and Death of a Rock Legend*. It Books, 2014. 247.

3. "About." *Woodstock*, 2020, woodstock.com. Accessed 3 Oct. 2019.

4. Roger Daltrey. *Thanks A Lot Mr. Kibblewhite: My Story.* Henry Holt and Company, 2018. 119.

CHAPTER 6. THE STRESS OF SUCCESS

1. Ben Marshall. *The Who: The Official History,* Harper Design, 2015. 177.

2. Roger Daltrey. *Thanks A Lot Mr. Kibblewhite: My Story.* Henry Holt and Company, 2018. 131.

3. Marshall, *The Who: The Official History,* 190.

4. Jake Abbate. "The Who's 'Lifehouse' Is Getting a Graphic Novel." *Superherohype*, 30 Mar. 2019, superherohype.com. Accessed 4 Oct. 2019.

5. Marshall, *The Who: The Official History,* 196.

SOURCE NOTES CONTINUED

CHAPTER 7. THE BIG SCREEN

1. Roger Daltrey. *Thanks A Lot Mr. Kibblewhite: My Story*. Henry Holt and Company, 2018. 175.

2. "Today in Music History: The Who Perform Loudest Concert in History." *The Current*, 31 May 2016, thecurrent.org. Accessed 5 Oct. 2019.

3. Dave Marsh. *Before I Get Old*. St. Martin's Press, 1983. 486.

4. Ken Sharp. "The Quiet One Speaks! A Chat with the Ox, The Who's John Entwistle." *Goldmine*, 5 July 1996, thewho.net. Accessed 14 Oct. 2019.

5. Dave Marsh. "Keith Moon: 1947–1978." *Rolling* Stone, 19 Oct. 1978, rollingstone.com. Accessed 15 Oct. 2019.

CHAPTER 8. *QUADROPHENIA* SAVES THE DAY

1. Ian Gilchrist. "We Are Still The Mods: Franc Roddam on Quadrophenia." *HeyUGuys*, 4 Nov. 2011, heyuguys.com. Accessed 7 Oct. 2019.

2. Dave Marsh. "Keith Moon: 1947–1978." *Rolling* Stone, 19 Oct. 1978, rollingstone.com. Accessed 15 Oct. 2019.

3. Marsh, "Keith Moon."

4. Chet Flippo. "Rock & Roll Tragedy: Why 11 Died at The Who's Cincinnati Concert." *Rolling Stone*, 24 Jan. 1980, rollingstone.com. Accessed 10 Oct. 2019.

5. Ben Marshall. *The Who: The Official History*. Harper Design, 2015. 274.

6. Marshall, *The Who: The Official History*, 272.

CHAPTER 9. GETTING THE BAND BACK TOGETHER

1. "January 1984." *The Who This Month*, n.d., thewhothismonth.com. Accessed 15 Oct. 2019.

2. "'Live Aid' Concert Raises $127 Million for Famine Relief in Africa." *History*, 27 July 2019, history.com. Accessed 9 Oct. 2019.

3. "'Live Aid' Concert Raises $127 Million for Famine Relief in Africa."

4. Martin Kielty. "15 Years Ago: The Who's John Entwistle Dies." *Ultimate Classic Rock*, 27 June 2017, ultimateclassicrock.com. Accessed 19 Sept. 2019.

5. Kielty, "15 Years Ago: The Who's John Entwistle Dies."

6. Andrew Grant Jackson. *1965: The Most Revolutionary Year in Music.* MacMillan, 2015. 208.

7. Martin Kielty. "The Who Announce New Album, 'Who.'" *Ultimate Classic Rock*, 13 Sept. 2019, ultimateclassicrock.com. Accessed 9 Oct. 2019.

8. Kielty, "The Who Announce New Album, 'Who.'"

INDEX

ABOUT THE AUTHOR

Sue Bradford Edwards

Sue Bradford Edwards is a Missouri nonfiction author who writes about culture and history, including the history of popular music. She is the author of 18 other titles from Abdo Publishing, including *The Murders of Tupac and Biggie*, *The Assassination of John F. Kennedy*, and *Hidden Human Computers*. Thanks to a friend who introduced her to the band's music, she listened to the Who throughout high school.